For The Champ
—T.B.

For Mr. Hollis King,
a friend, confidant, inspiration, and champ of my very own.
—R.G.C.

THIS IS A BORZOI BOOK PUBLISHED BY ALFRED A. KNOPF

TEXT COPYRIGHT © 2004 BY TONYA BOLDEN
ILLUSTRATIONS COPYRIGHT © 2004 BY R. GREGORY CHRISTIE
ALL RIGHTS RESERVED UNDER INTERNATIONAL AND PAN-AMERICAN COPYRIGHT CONVENTIONS.
PUBLISHED IN THE UNITED STATES BY ALFRED A. KNOPF, AN IMPRINT OF RANDOM HOUSE CHILDREN'S
BOOKS, A DIVISION OF RANDOM HOUSE, INC., NEW YORK, AND SIMULTANEOUSLY IN CANADA BY
RANDOM HOUSE OF CANADA LIMITED, TORONTO. DISTRIBUTED BY RANDOM HOUSE, INC., NEW YORK.

KNOPF, BORZOI BOOKS, AND THE COLOPHON ARE REGISTERED TRADEMARKS OF RANDOM HOUSE, INC.

WWW.RANDOMHOUSE.COM/KIDS

LIBRARY OF CONGRESS CATALOGING-IN-PUBLICATION DATA
BOLDEN, TONYA.
THE CHAMP! : THE STORY OF MUHAMMAD ALI /
BY TONYA BOLDEN ; ILLUSTRATED BY R. GREGORY CHRISTIE. — 1ST ED.
    P. CM.
ISBN 0-375-82401-4 (TRADE) — ISBN 0-375-92401-9 (LIB. BDG.)
1. ALI, MUHAMMAD, 1942– —JUVENILE LITERATURE. 2. BOXERS (SPORTS)—UNITED STATES—
BIOGRAPHY—JUVENILE LITERATURE. I. CHRISTIE, GREGORY, 1971– II. TITLE.
GV1132.A4B65 2004
796.83'092—DC22
2004010082

MANUFACTURED IN CHINA
DECEMBER 2004
10 9 8 7 6 5 4 3 2 1
FIRST EDITION

# THE CHAMP

**BY TONYA BOLDEN**

**ILLUSTRATED BY**
**R. GREGORY CHRISTIE**

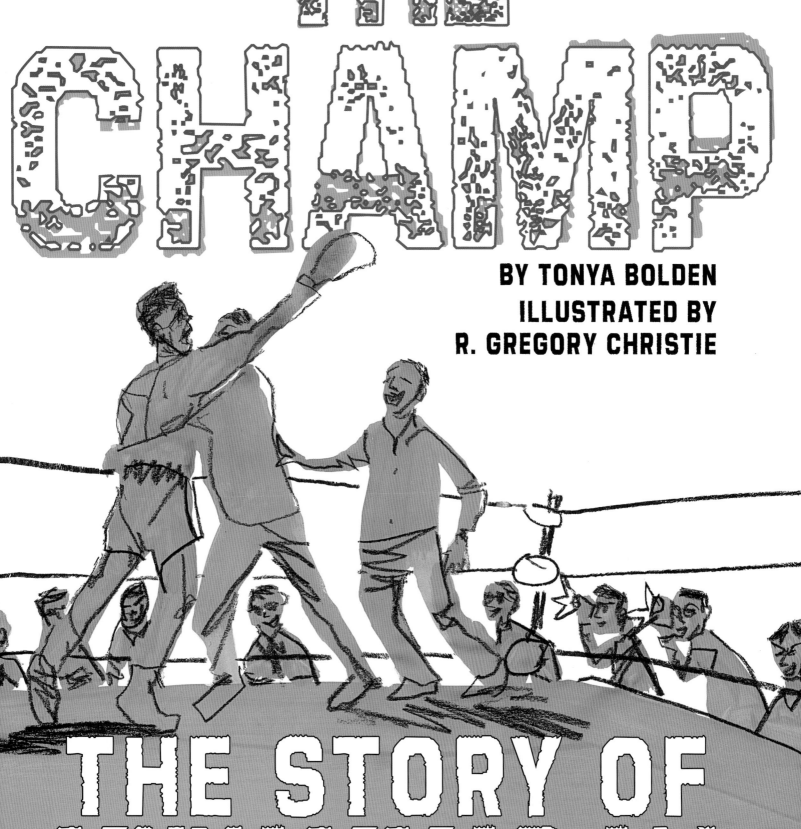

# THE STORY OF
# MUHAMMAD ALI

ALFRED A. KNOPF          NEW YORK

"Ali! **Ali! Ali!**"

**People still cheer him today.**

"**Ali! Ali!** Ali!"

All around the world—
in tall, gleaming cities,
in small, quiet towns—
the mere mention of the name
"Muhammad Ali"
will spark big smiles.

But Muhammad Ali was not always his name.

When he was born, on January 17, 1942, he was named after his daddy.

Cassius Marcellus Clay, Jr., was this Louisville, Kentucky, child's name.

Little Cassius talked a lot. He bossed a lot, too, as a tyke. "And by the time he was four, he had all the confidence in the world," his mama remembered.

When it came to play, Cassius developed a curious love for dodging rocks, remembered his brother, Rudy: "All the time, he used to ask me to throw rocks at him. I thought he was crazy, but he'd stand back and dodge every one of them. . . .

I could never hit him."

When he was twelve, what Cassius loved most was his red-and-white Schwinn. That sweet, swift Schwinn was his pride, the most beautiful thing in his life, his whizzzzzzzzzzz-around-Louisville delight—
being free,
**being fast,**
**having fun.**

Fun was all he thought about on the October day he rode his bike to an indoor fair.

When Cassius was ready to head home, all the day's fun—gone! Someone had swiped his Schwinn!

Cassius cried. Cassius was red-hot with rage inside. Thoughts of revenge against whoever had swiped his Schwinn raced around his mind.

"I'm gonna whup 'em!" That's what he was thinking when he reported the theft to Officer Joe Martin, off-duty down at the gym.

Officer Joe, who taught youngsters to box, couldn't see this string-beany boy whupping a stick. So he tossed the kid a tip: "You better learn how to fight before you start challenging people that you're gonna whup."

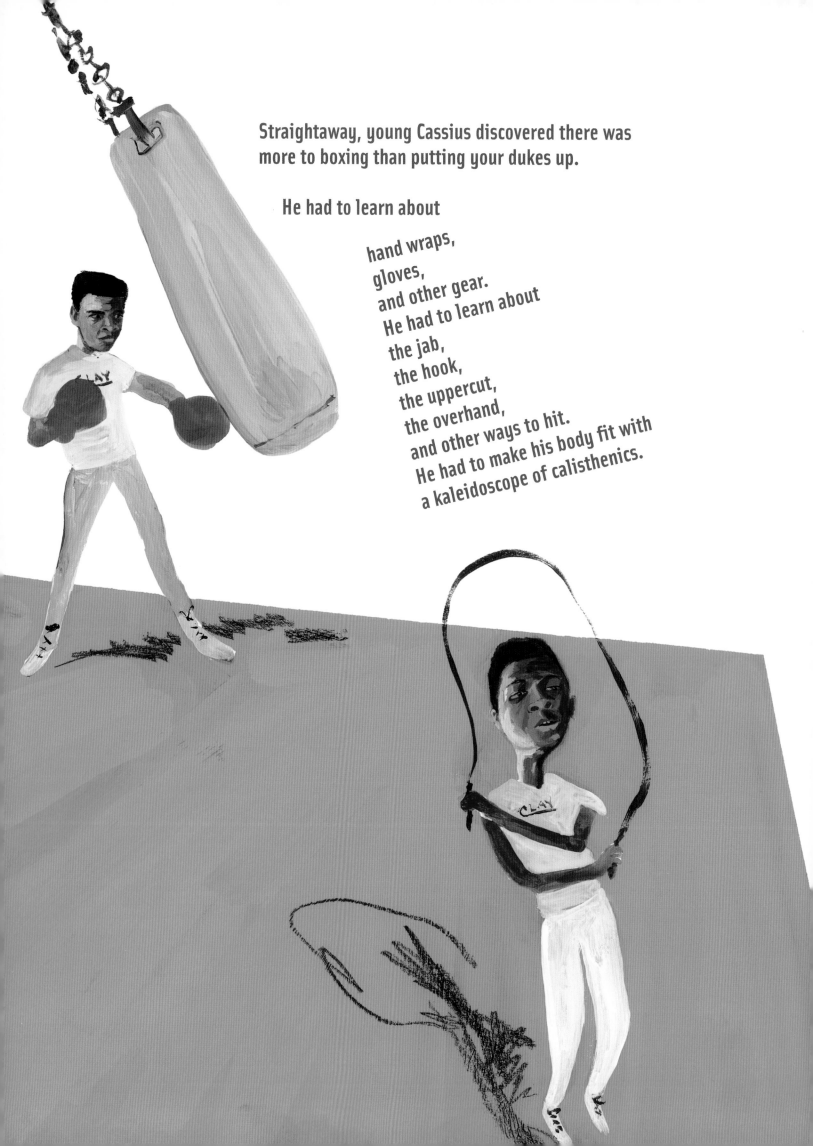

Straightaway, young Cassius discovered there was more to boxing than putting your dukes up.

He had to learn about

hand wraps,
gloves,
and other gear.
He had to learn about
the jab,
the hook,
the uppercut,
the overhand,
and other ways to hit.
He had to make his body fit with
a kaleidoscope of calisthenics.

In late 1954, Cassius had his first match—his first win!
Now his goal was to be a great boxer—
**the greatest!**—
to one day be **king of the ring:**

# THE CHAMP!

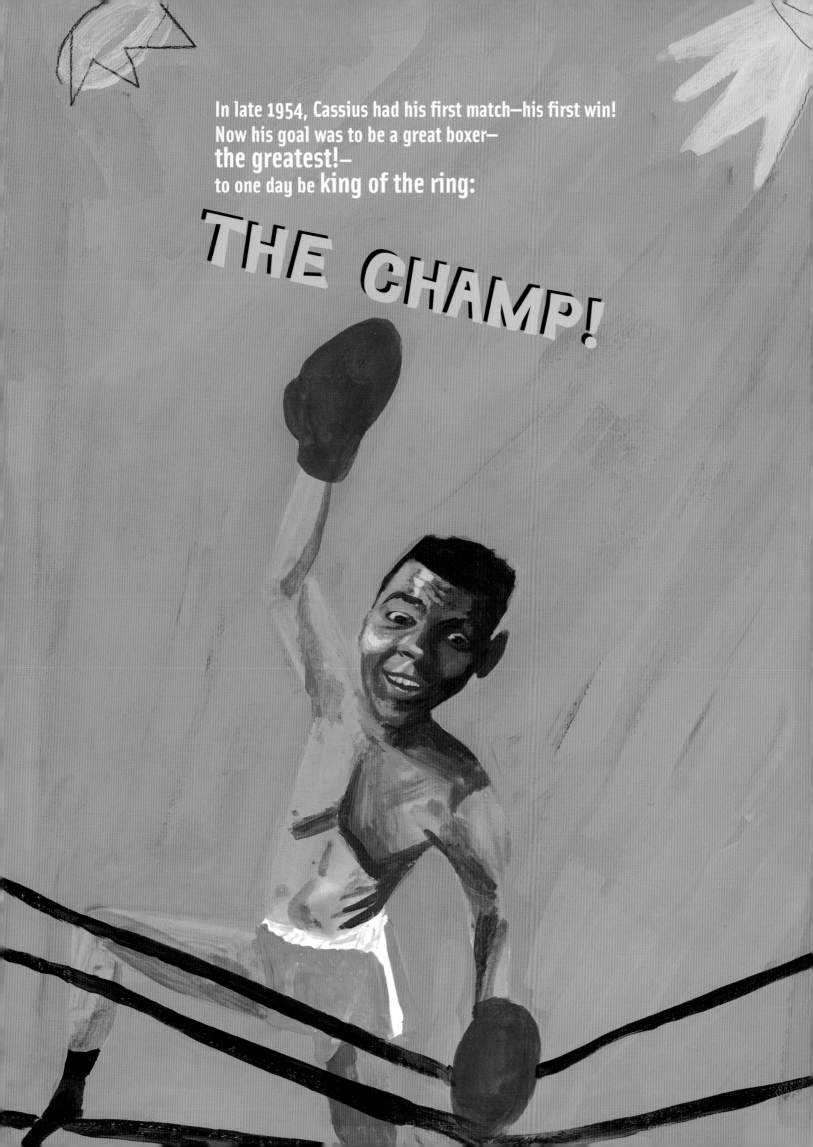

So Cassius stayed steady at the speed bag.
So Cassius hit, hit, hit hard at the heavy bag.

Early birds saw him
jogging, sprinting, running—

uphill,
downhill,
running through and around Chickasaw Park,
shadowboxing during some runs,
running forward,
running backward,
running sideways sometimes.
Monday,
Tuesday,
Wednesday,
Thursday,
Friday,
Saturday.
He was raised a Baptist. Sunday was his
Sabbath, the only day he did not train.

By age eighteen, Cassius Clay had won bout after bout and triumphed in several top tournaments. Then, in the summer of 1960, at the Olympic Games in Rome, Italy, he boxed his way to gold!

He wore his gold medal so proudly in Rome—and when he returned home to a hurricane of cheers. Not everyone was nice to him, though: When he walked into a Louisville luncheonette one day, he was told to get out. The man did not care that he was an Olympic champion. The man only cared that he was black.

But nothing kept young Cassius down; nothing hammered his hope of making it big in boxing. He bulked up to be a top-tier professional prizefighter: a heavyweight.

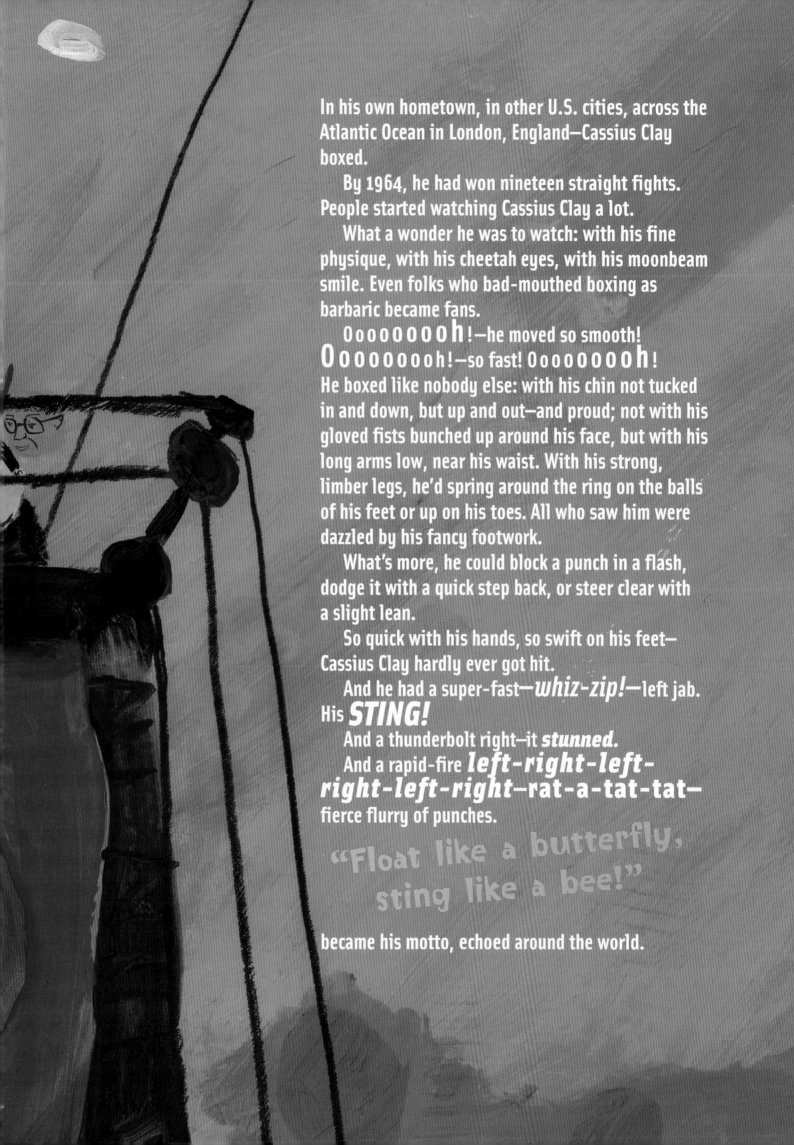

In his own hometown, in other U.S. cities, across the Atlantic Ocean in London, England—Cassius Clay boxed.

By 1964, he had won nineteen straight fights. People started watching Cassius Clay a lot.

What a wonder he was to watch: with his fine physique, with his cheetah eyes, with his moonbeam smile. Even folks who bad-mouthed boxing as barbaric became fans.

Oooooooooh!—he moved so smooth! Oooooooooh!—so fast! Oooooooooh! He boxed like nobody else: with his chin not tucked in and down, but up and out—and proud; not with his gloved fists bunched up around his face, but with his long arms low, near his waist. With his strong, limber legs, he'd spring around the ring on the balls of his feet or up on his toes. All who saw him were dazzled by his fancy footwork.

What's more, he could block a punch in a flash, dodge it with a quick step back, or steer clear with a slight lean.

So quick with his hands, so swift on his feet— Cassius Clay hardly ever got hit.

And he had a super-fast—*whiz-zip!*—left jab. His **STING!**

And a thunderbolt right—it *stunned.*

And a rapid-fire ***left-right-left-right-left-right***—rat-a-tat-tat— fierce flurry of punches.

"Float like a butterfly, sting like a bee!"

became his motto, echoed around the world.

**The Louisville Lip,**
**Mighty Mouth,**
**The Blabber**—these were some of the tags he picked
up along the way, because around reporters, in front
of cameras, or before a microphone, Cassius Clay sure
loved to talk, talk, talk—about his good looks,
about his excellence at fisticuffs.

Many a boast popped out as a poem, a rhyme, a rap.

"When you come to the fight,
don't block the aisle
and don't block the door.
You will all go home after round four."

That's what he declared before his fight with
Archie Moore—and sure enough, on November 15,
1962, in Los Angeles, California, Clay KO'd Moore in
round four.

"Clay swings with a left,
Clay swings with a right.
Look at young Cassius
carry the fight."

That's some of what Clay claimed when it came to
strongman Sonny Liston, who held the heavyweight
crown.

Most fight fans figured Liston would clobber Clay.
Liston thought so, too. He barely bothered to train
for their bout on February 25, 1964, in Miami Beach,
Florida.

The Louisville Lip lasted one round with Liston and then . . . a second, a third, a fourth, fifth, sixth—amazing fight fans with his speed, his skills, his strength—pummeling Liston all over the place.

**DING!**

There was no round seven. To everyone's amazement, Liston stayed slumped in his corner.

**"I AM THE GREATEST!"**

Cassius Clay hollered again and again.

**"I SHOOK UP THE WORLD!"**

Cassius Clay's highest hope had come true. He was—at last!—**king of the ring:**

**THE CHAMP!**

Two days later, he shocked the world again.

The Champ had become a Muslim. He had joined an American-born branch of that religion, the Nation of Islam.

Next came the news that The Champ had taken an Arabic name: Muhammad Ali.

Many people feared and despised the Nation of Islam because it preached that white people were devils. Deep down, The Champ did not see all whites as evil; he hated no one. What he hated was the way many whites treated blacks, from the days of slavery to the days in which he was living. The Champ did not hold back from talking about this, which made more people cheer him—and some people jeer him—as he went on to rack up more victories in the ring. Then, in the spring of 1967, he received an awful blow: drafted!

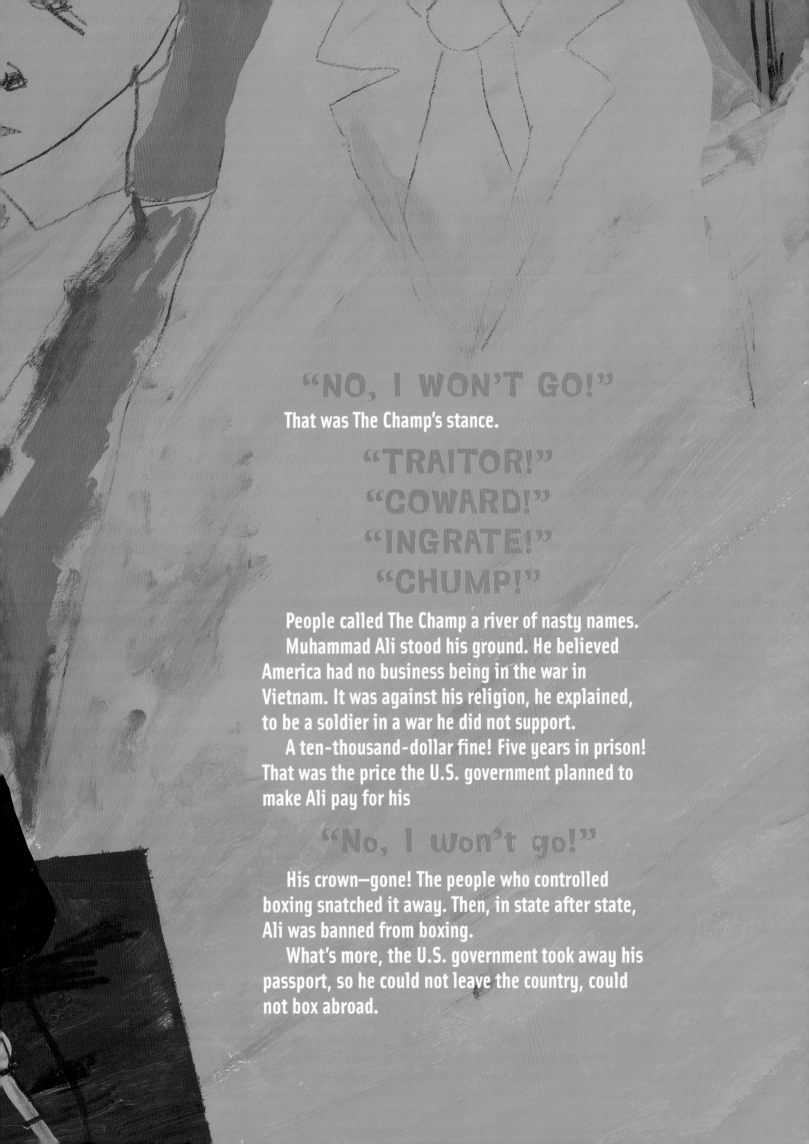

# "NO, I WON'T GO!"

That was The Champ's stance.

## "TRAITOR!"
## "COWARD!"
## "INGRATE!"
## "CHUMP!"

People called The Champ a river of nasty names. Muhammad Ali stood his ground. He believed America had no business being in the war in Vietnam. It was against his religion, he explained, to be a soldier in a war he did not support.

A ten-thousand-dollar fine! Five years in prison! That was the price the U.S. government planned to make Ali pay for his

### "No, I won't go!"

His crown—gone! The people who controlled boxing snatched it away. Then, in state after state, Ali was banned from boxing.

What's more, the U.S. government took away his passport, so he could not leave the country, could not box abroad.

"I would like to say to those of you who think I've lost so much, I have gained everything. I have peace of heart; I have a clear, free conscience. And I'm proud."

So said Ali in an address to college students. He was out on bail while his lawyers appealed his case.

Since he couldn't box, the main way Ali made a living was by giving talks: about his life, his beliefs, his hopes. He turned up, too, on talk shows, on game shows, and even on Broadway, starring in a play about black struggles and strengths.

He had such charisma! And not only that—people saw him as a great hero for standing up for his beliefs. So, day by day, month by month, love and support for Ali grew. Day by day, month by month, Ali prayed for a victory in the courts, and over the people who controlled his beloved sport.

One year passed, then another, and a third before Ali had his first great good news—he could box again!

October 26, 1970, was the date and Atlanta, Georgia, the place where Ali made his comeback. Once again, he climbed into the ring ready to float like a butterfly, sting like a bee. The great Jerry Quarry was trounced in round three.

"Ali! Ali! Ali!"

Several weeks later, against Oscar Bonavena—another win! And then—

"This might shock and amaze ya, but I'm gonna destroy Joe Frazier."

Joe Frazier, with his fidgety, frantic, frenzied fighting style, held the heavyweight crown.

Movie stars, singers—there were so many famous faces among the thousands packed into New York City's Madison Square Garden on March 8, 1971.

Round after round, Ali and Frazier hit each other hard. Never before had Ali been hit so many times. And . . .

Frazier kept the crown, stunning the crowd. Still, Ali kept believing that he could—he would!—once again be king of the ring, once again be

THE CHAMP!

In June 1971, Ali had a huge victory outside the ring. The U.S. Supreme Court ruled that he did not have to go to jail for saying no to the draft. The government had to return his passport, too.

**"Ali! Ali! Ali!"**

He was free—free from the threat of jail, free to box anywhere in the world.

More good news came soon.

By the fall of 1972, Ali had his own training camp in Deer Lake, Pennsylvania. "Muhammad Ali Welcomes You to Deer Lake" read the sign out front of his camp.

Old friends, new friends, total strangers—Muhammad Ali did not care who popped in. Almost always, he made time to chat and to give all who asked his autograph.

He loved people—all people. He shied away from no one: When a group of children with cerebral palsy came to Deer Lake, Ali kissed and hugged each and every one.

And he was as generous with his money as he was with his joy. With jokes, with wacky faces, with poems, rhymes, raps—he loved so much to make people laugh.

Sometimes, up popped a magic trick.

At Deer Lake—and wherever in the world he went—just being in Ali's presence made people feel special, precious—as if *they* were champs!

## "The bee has not lost his sting, and the butterfly still has his wings."

So said Ali after a loss to Ken Norton in late March 1973. And in a rematch several months later, Ali was the winner, as he was in his next two fights—the last one against that fidgety, frantic, frenzied Joe Frazier, who had lost the crown to fearsome George Foreman.

Ali faced Foreman in the fall of 1974. The "Rumble in the Jungle" is what people called that fight, though it did not take place in a jungle but in a soccer stadium in the city of Kinshasa, capital of Zaire.

"Ali! Ali! Ali!"

A huge crowd was there to greet Ali when he landed in Kinshasa.

"**Ali, bumbaye! Ali, bumbaye! Ali, bumbaye!**" That's what Ali heard almost everywhere he went. "Ali, destroy him!" is what the people were saying—but Foreman, boxing experts kept saying, was the most powerful puncher on the planet.

The heat! It was horribly hot the night of the Ali-
Foreman fight, with Foreman power-punching, with
Ali having a plan: to let Foreman wear himself out.
And sure enough, Foreman went weak; his punches,
slow, sloppy; his legs, wobbly.

DING!

In round eight, Ali sent Foreman
**stumbling,**
**tumbling**
**down.**

"Ali! Ali! Ali!"

The crowd went wild.
Ten years after he defeated strongman Sonny Liston—

"Ali! Ali! Ali!"

Seven years after his crown was snatched away—

"Ali! Ali! Ali!"

On October 30, 1974, Muhammad Ali was once again
king of the ring—THE CHAMP!
Even the African sky burst loose.

Muhammad Ali stayed king of the ring through his next ten fights. However, his sting had lost some of its whiz-zip. His reflexes were less than razor-sharp. His legs no longer let him spring around the ring as before. His hands were quick to get sore. With each fight, Ali got hit more and more.

Still, he boxed, once again going up against his old foe Frazier. October 1, 1975, was the date. Manila, capital of the Philippine Islands, the place.

The "Thrilla in Manila" is what people called this third, tougher, rougher Ali-Frazier fight.

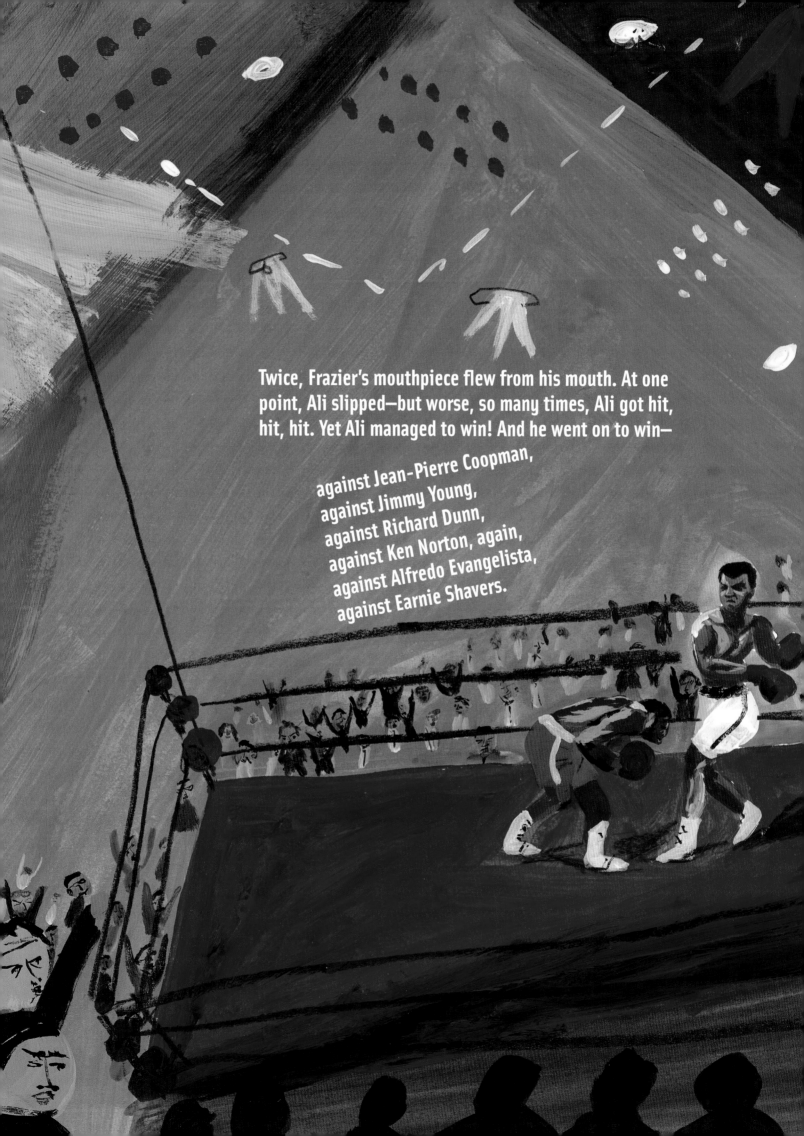

Twice, Frazier's mouthpiece flew from his mouth. At one point, Ali slipped—but worse, so many times, Ali got hit, hit, hit. Yet Ali managed to win! And he went on to win—

against Jean-Pierre Coopman,
against Jimmy Young,
against Richard Dunn,
against Ken Norton, again,
against Alfredo Evangelista,
against Earnie Shavers.

But against Leon Spinks, on February 15, 1978, in Las Vegas, Nevada, Ali lost his crown. Then, in a rematch seven months later, Ali had the victory! Ali made history! Never before had a boxer become The Champ one, two, three times!

"Ali! Ali! Ali!"

In the summer of 1979, Ali said good-bye to boxing. Then, in October 1980, he was back in the ring, in Las Vegas, Nevada, against Larry Holmes. For the first time in his professional career, Ali was

TKO'D

In time, it became clear that Ali had lost much more than his excellence at fisticuffs.

There was a tremble to his hands. To his speech, a slur. His walk was far from limber, but stiff. Muhammad Ali had boxed for too long; he had taken too many blows, especially to the head.

The ailing Ali did not hide from view. Instead, he put his fame to good use: He traveled the world, speaking for peace between nations and among the races, spotlighting the plight of the needy, spreading his joy. A crowd still formed in a flick wherever he went. Autograph after autograph, just as before, Ali rarely said no. Plus, he still had his kit of magic tricks.

"Ali! Ali! Ali!"

Muhammad Ali was the big surprise at the 1996 Summer Olympics—the 100th anniversary of the Games—held that year in Atlanta, Georgia. Ali had the high honor of touching the Olympic torch to the cauldron, with its flame signaling the start of the Games.

Thousands in the stadium, plus three billion in front of TV's, watched in awe as Ali tackled his task: so stiff, so slow, so trembly. And so, showing the world he was greater than his ailment. And so, inspiring others to believe they, too, could triumph over troubles.

"Ali! Ali! Ali!"

Yes, people still cheer him today.

His face, his name,
his days of trials and glories,
his courage inside and outside the ring—
children the world over learn of his story year after year.
And they hear that for many,
Muhammad Ali
will always be

# THE CHAMP!

## NOTES

"And . . . all the confidence in the world." Odessa Clay, quoted in Hauser, *Muhammad Ali: His Life and Times*, 16.

"All the time . . . never hit him." Rudolph Clay, quoted in Hauser, *Muhammad Ali: His Life and Times*, 17.

"You . . . gonna whup." Joe Martin, quoted in Hauser, *Muhammad Ali: His Life and Times*, 18.

"When you come . . . round four." Cassius Clay, quoted in Remnick, 122.

"Clay swings . . . the fight." Cassius Clay, quoted in Remnick, 148.

"I am . . . world." Cassius Clay (who changed his name to Muhammad Ali in March 1964), quoted in Remnick, 200.

"I would like to say . . . I'm proud." Muhammad Ali, quoted in Hauser, *Muhammad Ali in Perspective*, 19.

"This might shock . . . Joe Frazier." Muhammad Ali, quoted in Hauser, *Muhammad Ali: His Life and Times*, 222.

"The bee has . . . wings." Muhammad Ali, in an interview excerpted in *Muhammad Ali: The Whole Story*, vol. 4.

## SELECTED SOURCES

Hauser, Thomas. *Muhammad Ali: His Life and Times*. New York: Simon & Schuster, 1991.

———, with the cooperation of Muhammad Ali. *Muhammad Ali in Perspective*. San Francisco: HarperCollins, 1996.

Miller, Davis. *The Tao of Muhammad Ali*. New York: Three Rivers Press, 1999.

*Muhammad Ali: The Whole Story*. Vol. 1–6. VHS. Turner Home Video, 2001.

*Muhammad Ali: Through the Eyes of the World*. VHS. Universal Studios, 2002.

Remnick, David. *King of the World: Muhammad Ali and the Rise of an American Hero*. New York: Vintage, 1999.